I0789167

The Story of a Special Day
Volume 166

June
14

The 165th day of the year (166th in leap years). There are 200 days remaining until the end of the year.

by Michael Dobson

Timespinner
Press

This book is also available in e-book form for Kindle, e-pub devices, and other formats from your favorite online booksellers.

For more information about the series, about us, or about your special day, please email us at editor@timespinnerpress.com.

Look for other volumes in *The Story of a Special Day*, coming often. See www.timespinnerpress.com for details and for the most recent information.

Table of Contents

Cover: Detail from the painting "Betsy Ross 1777" by Jean Leon Gerome Ferris. Although Betsy Ross almost certainly didn't make the first US flag, the US Congress adopted the "Stars and Stripes" June 14, 1777, celebrated as FLAG DAY — the COVER STORY.

Quote of the Day

"Fiction has to be plausible. All history has to do is happen."

Harry Turtledove, historian and novelist
born June 14, 1949

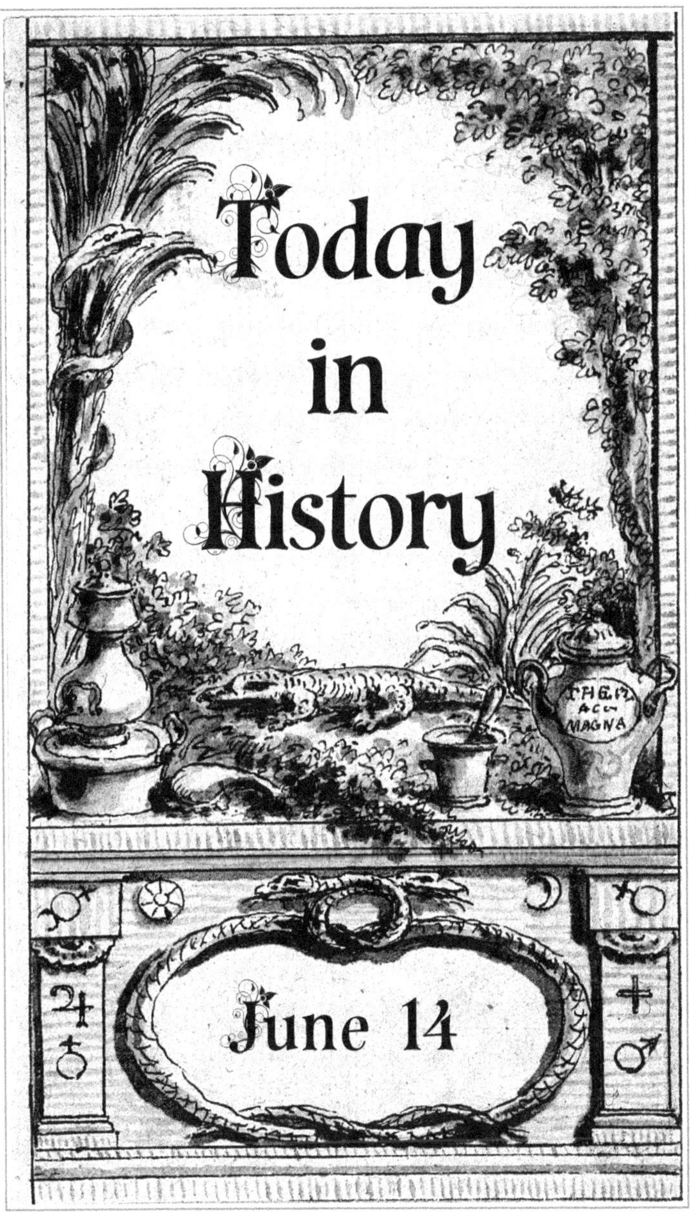
Today
in
History

THERIACA MAGNA

June 14

The mutineers on HMS *Bounty* set Captain Bligh and loyal members of his crew adrift. (Credit: National Maritime Museum, Greenwich, London)

Alcock and Brown and their Vickers Vimy prior to their successful transatlantic flight, June 14, 1919

What Happened on June 14?

From the creation of great works of engineering and art, to devastating wars and natural disasters, thousands of years of history have left their mark on each and every day of the year. Here are some additional important events that occurred on June 14. (Illustrated items are shaded.)

1775 — During the **American Revolutionary War**, the Continental Congress establishes the Continental Army. The US Army celebrates this date as its official birthday.

1789 — Following the **Mutiny on the Bounty**, Captain William Bligh and 18 of his crewmen arrive safely in Timor after a 43-day, 3,500 mile journey in an open boat.

1800 — In the Battle of Marengo, the army of First Consul **Napoleon Bonaparte** defeats an Austrian force and reconquers Italy in his first major victory following his successful *coup d'état* the previous year.

1807 — In the Battle of Friedland, **Emperor Napoleon I** achieves a decisive victory over Russia, ending the War of the Fourth Coalition.

1900 — **Hawaii** becomes a US territory.

1919 — British aviators John Alcock and Arthur Brown set off on the **first nonstop transatlantic flight,** landing in a bog in Ireland the following day.

1940 — The first mass transport of prisoners to the **Auschwitz** concentration camp takes place.

1949 — Rhesus monkey Albert II is launched on a V-2 rocket and becomes the **first monkey in space**, although he dies on impact after a parachute failure.

1954 — US President Dwight D. Eisenhower signs a bill to add the words "under God" to the **Pledge of Allegience**.

1959 — The **Disneyland Monorail System**, the first daily operating monorail in the Western Hemisphere, opens.

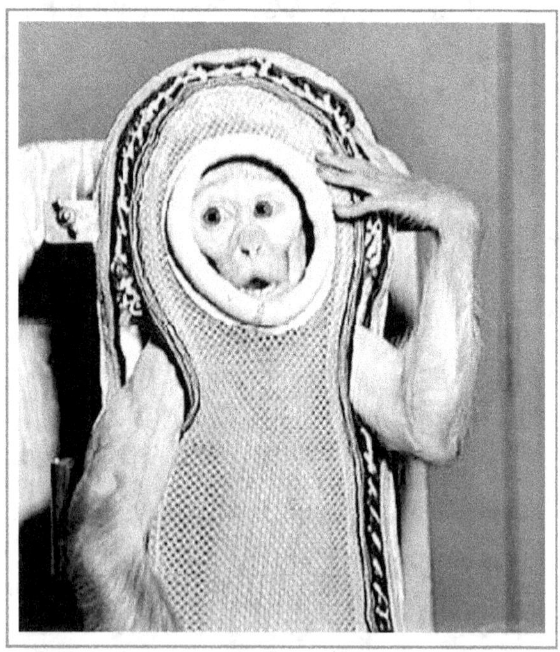

A rhesus monkey prior to being launched into space.

Disneyland Monorail System (Photo: David Jones, CC BY SA 2.0)

Quote of the Day

"The longest day must have its close — the gloomiest night will wear on to a morning. An eternal, inexorable lapse of moments is ever hurrying the day of the evil to an eternal night, and the night of the just to an eternal day."

Harriet Beecher Stowe, author of *Uncle Tom's Cabin*
born June 14, 1811

Births
and
Deaths
THER
ACA
MAGNA
June 14

Harriet Beecher Stowe, author of *Uncle Tom's Cabin*. Stowe was
born June 14, 1811

Notable June 14 People

With the current world population at about seven billion people, on average about 19 million people also celebrate their birthdays on June 14 — and that isn't counting the millions and millions who came before! No matter when you were born, you share your birthday with many special people whose accomplishments (and occasionally embarrassments) have been noted as part of history.

In this section, you'll meet fascinating people who share your birthday. They're organized by what they're famous for, and then in reverse chronological order from most recent to earliest. Those who are shown in photographs or artwork have a box around them. We don't have photos of everyone, so please forgive us if your favorite person is missing.

Some of these people you've heard of, others may be new to you, but they all make up an important part of the reason that June 14 is a truly special day!

Donald Trump, 45th US President, born June 14, 1936 (Credit: USAF SSGT Jette Carr)

Who Was Born on June 14?

Art and Photography

Arthur Davis, animator and director for Warner Brothers cartoons, including Bugs Bunny. *(1905)*

Margaret Bourke-White, first female war photojournalist, working in combat zones during World War II. She was also the first female photographer for *Life* Magazine, and the first foreign photographer allowed to take pictures of Soviet industry. She was portrayed by Candice Bergen in the 1982 film *Gandhi* and by Farrah Fawcett in 1989's *Double Exposure: The Story of Margaret Bourke-White.* *(1904)*

"Kentucky Flood," iconic photo by Margaret Bourke-White, 1937

Government and Politics

Donald Trump, real estate magnate and host of the television reality series *The Apprentice,* elected 45th President of the United States in 2016. *(1936) (Photo page 10.)*

Joe Arpaio, controversial lawman who billed himself as "America's Toughest Sheriff" for his crackdowns on illegal immigration. Repeatedly accused of misconduct including unlawful enforcement and racial profiling; convicted of criminal contempt of court in 2017 for which he was pardoned by US President Donald Trump. *(1932)*

Che Guevara, Argentine Marxis revolutionary and guerrila leader and a major figure in the Cuban Revolution. *(1928)*

Robert M. La Follette Sr., Wisconsin progressive politician known as "Fighting Bob;" ran unsuccessfully as the Progressive Party candidate for US President in 1924, named one of the "five greatest US Senators" by the US Senate itself. *(1855)*

Journalism and Literature

Campbell Brown, television journalist and anchorwoman of the NBC program *Weekend Today* and host of the CNN series Campbell Brown. *(1968)*

Che Guevara

Mona Simpson, award-winning novelist known for her debut novel *Anywhere but Here*; younger sister of Apple CEO and co-founder Steve Jobs. *(1957)*

Harry Turtledove, American historical, fantasy, and science fiction novelist known as the "Master of Alternate History." *(1949)*

Jerzy Kosiński, author of *The Painted Bird* and *Being There*, the latter adapted into an Academy Award-winning film. *(1931)*

Pierre Salinger, White House press secretary under John F. Kennedy, later a US senator and a television news correspondent. *(1925)*

Lise Nørgaard, Danish writer who wrote the 1992 best-seller *Kun en Pige (Only a Girl)*, made into a feature film; creator and co-host of the long-running Danish television series *Matador*. *(1917)*

John Bartlett, writer and publisher best known for *Bartlett's Familiar Quotations*. *(1820)*

Harriet Beecher Stowe, abolitionist and writer, best known for her 1852 novel *Uncle Tom's Cabin*. *(1811)* *(Photo page 8.)*

Music

Boy George, singer-songwriter best known as lead singer of the pop band Culture Club; hits include "Do You Really Want to Hurt Me" and "Karma Chameleon." *(1961)*

Alan White, English drummer and songwriter best known as a member of the progressive rock band Yes; member of the Rock and Roll Hall of Fame. *(1949)*

Rod Argent, singer-songwriter and producer known as the founder and keyboardist of the rock band The Zombies, for which he wrote "She's Not There" and "Time of the Season," and for his subsequent solo career. *(1945)*

Renaldo Benson, singer-songwriter best known as a member of The Four Tops; co-wrote "What's Going On;" member of the Rock and Roll Hall of Fame. *(1936)*

Junior Walker, musician best known for leading the Motown group Jr. Walker & the All Stars, whose signature song is the 1965 hit "Shotgun." *(1931)*

Cy Coleman, composer and songwriter whose hits include "Witchcraft," "Hey, Look Me Over," "If My Friends Could See Me Now," and numerous film scores. *(1929)*

Performing Arts

Diablo Cody, won the Academy Award for Best Original Screenplay for the 2007 film *Juno;* created and produced the Showtime television series *United States of Tara. (1978)*

Alan Carr, English comedian and television talk show host. *(1976)*

Paul O'Grady, English comedian and television personality initially known for his drag queen character "Lily Savage" and for his long-running daytime talk show, *The Paul O'Grady Show. (1931)*

Marla Gibbs, actress best known for playing George Jefferson's maid Florence in the sitcom *The Jeffersons,* for which she received five Emmy nominations. *(1931)*

Sam Wanamaker, actor and director who left the US to avoid being blacklisted; credited as person most responsible for the recreation of Shakepeare's Globe Theatre. Had roles in the films *Private Benjamin, Superman IV,* and *Baby Boom,* among others. *(1919)*

Gene Barry, actor best known for playing the title characters in the television series *Bat Masterson* and *Burke's Law. (1919) (Photo page 15.)*

Dorothy McGuire, nominated for the Best Actress Oscar for the 1947 film *Gentlemen's Agreement. (1916)*

Burl Ives, singer and actor best known for films such as *Cat on a Hot Tin Roof* and *The Big Country* (winning an Academy Award for the latter), and as the voice of "Sam the Snowman" on the holiday perennial *Rudolph the Red-Nosed Reindeer. (1909) (Photo page 18.)*

Gene Barry as Bat Masterson

Burl Ives (Photo: Carl Van Vechten

May Allison, Broadway and silent film star best known for her popular films with Harold Lockwood. *(1890)*

May Allison (right) with Harold Lockwood in *Big Tremaine* (1916)

Religion and Philosophy

Rowan Williams, Archbishop of Canterbury and Primate of All England; made a baron and elevated to the House of Lords following his retirement. *(1950)*

Science and Medicine

James Black, received the 1988 Nobel Prize in Physiology or Medicine for the development of the drugs propranolol and cimetidine. *(1924)*

Jacob Ellehammer, Danish watchmaker and inventor who built the first air-cooled radial engine, which he used to power a successful triplane and helicopter in the early years of aviation. *(1871)*

Jacob Ellehammer's triplane (1907)

Karl Landsteiner, received the 1930 Nobel Prize in Physiology or Medicine for development of the modern system of classifying blood groups; known as the "father of transfusion medicine." *(1868)*

Alois Alzheimer, German psychiatrist and neuropathologist who identified the first published case of "presenile dementia," later named Alzheimer's disease. *(1864)*

Andrey Markov (Андре́евич Ма́рков), Russian mathematician best known for his work on stochastic processes, including Markov chains. *(1736)*

Charles-Augustin de Coulomb, French physicist known for developing Coulomb's Law The unit of electric charge, the coulomb, is named for him. *(1736)*

Sports

Steve Bégin, ice hockey centre who played 13 seasons in the NHL; won the Jack A. Butterfield Trophy in 2001 as the most valuable player in the Calder Cup championship playoffs. *(1978)*

Steffi Graf, German tennis player ranked World No 1 for a record-setting 377 weeks; only tennis player to win all four Grand Slam titles and the Olympic gold medal in the same calendar year; member of the Tennis Hall of Fame. *(1969) (Photo page 22.)*

Éric Desjardins, played 17 seasons in the National Hockey League with the Montreal Canadiens and the Philadelphia Flyers, winning the Stanley Cup with Montreal in 1993. *(1969)*

Steffi Graf (Photo: Chris Eason, CC BY-SA 2.0)

Samuel Perkins, three-time college All-American and USA Baskeball Male Athlete of the Year; won a gold medal as co-captain of the 1984 US Olympic basketball team. *(1961)*

Pat Summitt, women's college basketball head coach for the Tennessee Lady Vols who accrued the most career wins in NCAA basketball history; first to achieve 1,000 wins; won two Olympic medals in basketball, a gold as coach and a silver as player. Named Naismith Basketball Coach of the Century and awarded the Presidential Medal of Freedom. *(1952)*

Richard Stebbins, American athlete who won a gold medal at the 1964 Tokyo Olympics in the 4x100m relay; subsequently a wide receiver for the New York Giants. *(1945)*

Don Newcombe, pitcher for the Dodgers, Reds and Indians, first black pitcher to start a World Series game, and first pitcher of any race to win the National League MVP and the Cy Young Award in the same season. *(1926)*

Jack Adams, only person to win the Stanley Cup as a player, coach, and general manager; member of the Hockey Hall of Fame. *(1894)*

 Michael Dobson

Self-Portrait, Mary Cassatt (1878)

Who Died on June 14?

Art and Design

Mary Cassatt, American painter and printmaker known for her Impressionist paintings and for her relationship with Edgar Degas. *(1926)*

William Le Baron Jenney, American architect who built the first skyscraper in 1884; known as the "father of the American skyscraper." *(1907)*

The Home Insurance Building, Chicago, designed by William Le Baron Jenney

Pierre Charles L'Enfant, engineer and urban planner famous for designing the plan for the new capital city of the United States, Washington, DC. *(1825)*

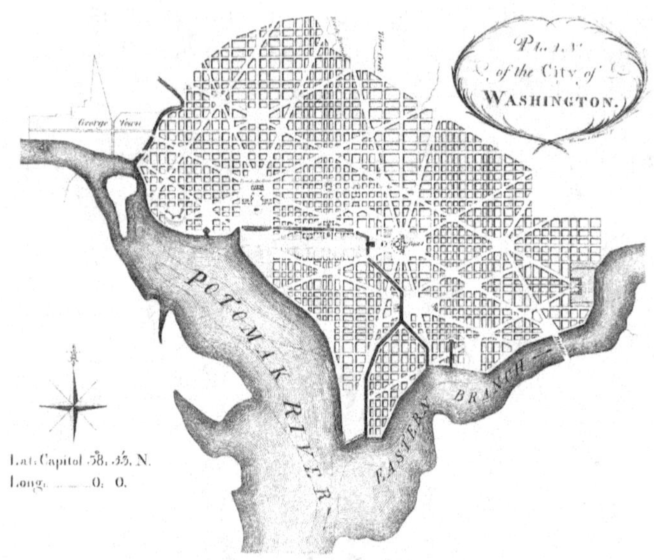

Pierre L'Enfant's plan for the city of Washington, DC, 1792

Government and Politics

Kurt Waldheim, former Secretary-General of the United Nations and President of Austria; later revealed as a former Nazi intelligence officer suspected of war crimes. *(2007)*

Emmeline Pankhurst, British political activist and leader of the suffragette movement; named by Time magazine as one of the "100 Most Important People of the 20th Century" for her crucial role in achieving women's suffrage in Britain. *(1928)*

Emmeline Pankhurst is arrested for trying to present a petition for women's suffrage to King George V, May 21, 1914

Adlai Stevenson I, 23ʳᵈ Vice President of the United States; grandfather of Illinois Governor Adlai Stevenson II, unsuccessful presidential candidate in 1952 and 1956. *(1914)*

Journalism and Literature

Roger Zelazny, science fiction and fantasy writer who won three Nebula Awards and six Hugo Awards; known for such works as *The Chronicles of Amber, Lord of Light, This Immortal,* and "A Rose for Ecclesiastes." *(1995)*

Jose Luis Borges, Argentine author in the magic realism tradition; major works include *Ficciones, El Aleph,* and *A Universal History of Infamy. (1986)*

Salvatore Quasimodo, Italian novelist and poet who won the 1959 Nobel Prize for Literature. *(1968)*

G. K. Chesterton, English writer best known for his *Father Brown* mysteries and for his 1908 novel *The Man Who Was Thursday. (1936)*

Jerome K. Jerome, English writer and humorist best known for the 1889 travelogue *Three Men in a Boat* and his 1886 essay collection *Idle Thoughts of an Idle Fellow. (1883)*

Edward FitzGerald, English poet best known for his translation of *The Rubaiyat of Omar Khayyam. (1883)*

Military

Benedict Arnold, general in the Continental Army during the American Revolutionary War who defected to the British and attempted to surrender the fortifications at West Point to British forces; subsequently a general in the British army. His name is often used in America as a synonym for "traitor." *(1801)*

Benedict Arnold, by Henry Bryan Hall

Music

Bob Bogle, founder, lead guitarist, and later bassist of The Ventures; played lead guitar on the 1960 hit "Walk, Don't Run;" member of the Rock and Roll Hall of Fame. *(2009)*

The Ventures (left to right): **Bob Bogle**, Nokie Edwards, Mel Taylor, Don Wilson

Rory Gallagher, Irish blues and rock multi-instrumentalist and songwriter who sold more than 30 million albums worldwide. *(1995)*

Henry Mancini, composer who won four Academy Awards and twenty Grammys; best known works include "The Pink Panther Theme," "Moon River," and "Baby Elephant Walk." *(1994)*

Performing Arts

Ann Guilbert, actress best known as Millie on *The Dick Van Dyke Show* and Yetta on *The Nanny. (2016)*

Elroy Schwartz, screenwriter best known as head writer for *Gilligan's Island*, created by his brother Sherwood. *(2013)*

Richard Jaeckel, actor in such films as *Sometimes a Great Notion* and *The Dirty Dozen*, also known as Lt. Edwards on the television series *Baywatch. (1994)*

Dame Peggy Ashcroft, English stage and screen actress who appeared in the television miniseries *The Jewel in the Crown* and had an Oscar-winning role in 1985's *A Passage to India. (1991)*

Alan Jay Lerner, lyricist and librettist known for his partnership with Frederick Loewe; best known plays include *Brigadoon, Paint Your Wagon, Royal Wedding, An American in Paris, My Fair Lady*, and many others. Won three Academy Awards and three Tony Awards for his work. *(1986)*

Religion and Philosophy

Max Weber, German philosopher and political economist considered one of the three founders of the discipline of sociology. *(1920)*

Abu Hanifa (أبو حنيفة نعمان بن ثابت بن زوطا بن مرزبان), renowned Islamic scholar who founded the Hanafi school of orthodox Sunni jurisprudence, considered one of the greatest legal philosophers of all time. *(772)*

Science and Technology

John Logie Baird, Scottish engineer and inventor who demonstrated the first working television system in 1926 and who invented the first publicly demonstrated color television system. *(1946)*

Sports

Bob Chappuis, member of the College Football Hall of Fame as a halfback and quarterback for the University of Michigan Wolverines; flew 21 missions as a radioman and gunner on B-25s in Europe during World War II. *(2012)*

Ottavio Bottecchia, first Italian winner of the Tour de France who died mysteriously; some claim he was assassinated by the Mussolini regime for anti-fascist leanings. *(1927)*

John Logie Baird and his first publicly demonstrated television system, featuring ventriloquist dummy "Stooky Bill," 1925 (Credit: Orrin Dunlap, Jr., *Popular Radio* magazine)

Quote of the Day

"It is always the best policy to speak the truth, unless, of course, you are an exceptionally good liar."

Jerome K. Jerome, English author and humorist
born June 14, 1927

Holidays
Around
the World

June 14

A 1917 poster for Flag Day — for **FLAG DAY IN THE UNITED STATES,** celebrated June 14

June 14 Holidays and Celebrations

If you're looking for a reason to take your special day off, you should know that every single day is a holiday somewhere in the world! Here's some of what you can celebrate on June 14!

Cover Story
Flag Day in the United States

Many nations set aside a day each year to honor their national flag. In the United States, Flag Day commemorates the Flag Resolution, adopted by the Second Continental Congress on June 14, 1777. It read, "Resolved, That the flag of the thirteen United States be thirteen stripes, alternate red and white; that the union by thirteen stars, white in a blue field, representing a new constellation."

The first American flag, the "Continental Colors," had the familiar thirteen alternating red and white stripes, but had the British Union Flag in the upper left corner. It was first raised by Lieutenant John Paul Jones of the Continental Navy on December 3, 1775. At that time, flags were primarily used by the military, and the concept of a "national flag" was relatively new.

After some debate, the Second Continental Congress decided to keep the stripes, but replace the Union Jack with thirteen stars. They didn't specify any particular arrangement of the stars or the order of the stripes, so there were a number of variations.

The story that Betsy Ross sewed the first flag from a pencil sketch given to her by George Washington has been widely discredited by historians. Ross was an upholsterer, not a seamstress, and had never made a flag. Plus, the story says she made the flag in the spring of 1776, more than a year before it became official.

Some credit Rebecca Young with making the first flag. She was actually a flag-maker, and made quite a number of early flag, whether or not she created the first. With her daughter, Mary Young Pickersgill, she sewed the flag that flew over Ft. McHenry during the War of 1812 and inspired the writing of "The Star-Spangled Banner."

The official design of the flag is credited to naval flag designer Francis Hopkinson, who submitted a bill for "a Quarter Cask of the Public Wine" as payment for designing the flag and the Great Seal of the United States, among other things. He didn't get the wine, because he was a member of Congress and already received a salary for his work.

As states were added to the Union, the flag had to change. When Vermont and Kentucky were admitted, the flag changed to 15 stars and 15 stripes. Adding more stripes became problematic, though additional stars were not a problem, so in 1818, the flag design was changed to have one star per state but a limit of 13 stripes for the 13 original colonies.

The current 50-star US flag is the 27th official version, and has been in effect since July 1960, when Alaska and Hawaii were admitted as states. It is now the longest-used version of the US flag.

Flag etiquette is established by the United State Flag Code, which has guidelines of the use, display, and disposal of the flag.

Flag Day was first established on a national level by proclamation of President Woodrow Wilson in 1916, although local and unofficial Flag Days had been celebrated in several states. Congress made National Flag Day a permanent institution in 1946. Flag Day is part of National Flag Week (held whichever week containe June 14 in a particular year). Citizens are urged to fly the American Flag, and some cities and towns hold Flag Day parades.

The first **Flag Day** (1919)

General Events

Commemoration of the Soviet Deportation from the Baltic States (various nations)

Just before the invasion of the Soviet Union by Nazi Germany, the Soviet government began a series of deportations of "anti-Soviet elements" in the Baltic states and elsewhere. These deportations lasted from May 22 to June 20, 1941, involving at least 85,000 people. Among Estonian deportees alone, around 60% died in prison camps or through forced resettlement.

The deportation is commemorated in several nations on June 14, including:

- **Baltic Freedom Day**, United States
- *Leinapäev* (Day of Mourning and Commemoration), Estonia
- **Mourning and Hope Day**, Lithuania

Father's Day (numerous nations)

While different countries may set aside different days to honor fathers, many nations, including the US, UK, Japan, Mexico, China, India, and Pakistan, celebrate on the third Sunday in June.

Freedom Day (Malawi)

The African nation of Malawi celebrates Freedom Day on the anniversary of its first free election, June 14, 1994.

Neckties and cookies are traditional **Father's Day** gifts, though not usually combined. (Photo: Dean Michaud, CC BY-SA 2.0)

Liberation Day (Falkland Islands)

The British overseas territory of the Falkland Islands celebrates the end of the Falklands War (*Guerra de las Malvinas*) between the United Kingdom and Argentina over control of the Falkland Islands and the South Sandwich Islands/South Georgia. The war ended after 74 days with a British victory.

World Blood Donor Day (international)

The UN's World Health Organization raises awareness for the need for safe blood and blood products and thanks blood donors on June 14 each year.

The date commemorates the 1868 birth of Karl Landsteiner, an Austrian immunologist who developed the modern system for classifying blood groups, for which he received a Nobel Prize.

Religious Feast Days and Holidays

Trinity Sunday (western Christianity)

In western Christianity, the doctrine of the Trinity is observed the first Sunday after Pentecost. The date varies between May 17 and June 20.

Saint Days

Each day in the year is considered a feast day for one or more saints. They are somewhat different in western Christianity (Catholicism and many forms of Protestantism) and in eastern (Orthodox) Christianity. There are many others; this is a selection.

In *Western Christianity*, June 14 is the feast day of the Prophet Elisha and Saints Burchard of Meissen, Caomhán of Inisheer, the, Joseph the Hymnographer, Methodius I of Constantinople, Quinitan of Rodez, Richard Baxter (Church of England), and Valerius and Rufinus.

In *Eastern Orthodox Christianity*, it is also the commemoration of Saints John of Euchaita, Niphon of Mount Athos, Prince Mstislav-George of Novgorod, Elisha of Sumsk in Solovki, Methodius of Peshnosha, Julitta of Tabenna, and Joseph of Thessalonica. (These saints are honored on June 27 by "Old Calendrists.*")

---

* "Old Calendrists" use the older Julian calendar rather than the modern Gregorian calendar for liturgical purposes. For more about the different types of calendars, see "What Day of the Week is June 14?"

Moveable and Multi-Day Events

Some events take place over a specific week or time period. Start and finish dates may vary from year to year. Some events occur on different days each year (such as "fourth Saturday of a month"). These events sometimes take place on or include June 14.

Beginning of the Hindu month of Mithuna (mid-June)

- *Raja Parba* (ରଜ ପର୍ବ), three-day festival to mark the beginning of the agricultural year in the Indian state of Odisha

Varies between March and July

- *Phi Ta Khon*, also known as the Ghost Festival, is a three-day Buddhist celebration in Loei province, Thailand. The date is selected annually by each town's spirit mediums.

Week Including June 12

- National Automotive Service Professionals Week (US)

Monday after the Second Saturday

- Queen's Official Birthday (Norfolk Island)

Second Tuesday

- Call Your Doctor Day (US)
- World Pet Memorial Day (international)

Celebrations About Food

In the United States, almost every day of the year is dedicated to a particular food — some days honor more than one!. Sponsored by manufacturers, retailers, farmers, or simply fans, these days are often proclaimed by the President, Congress, state governors, or mayors.

In the US, June 14 is **National Strawberry Shortcake Day.** Shortcake is a crumbly sweet biscuit, usually leavened with baking soda or baking powder, although many "shortcakes" are made with sponge cake instead. In some places, it's made from pie crust or from broken-up pieces of pie crust. No matter which type of base is used, it's always topped with strawberries and whipped cream.

You can top your shortcake with other fruits, including peaches, blueberries and (though it's not a fruit) chocolate.

Although it's not technically a food, June 14 is also **National Bourbon Day**. Whether that's before or after the shortcake is up to you.

The whole month of June is set aside to honorthe following foods.

- Georgia Blueberry Month
- National Candy Month
- National Dairy Month
- National Fresh Fruit and Vegetables Month
- National Iced Tea Month
- National Papaya Month

A strawberry shortcake, for **National Strawberry Shortcake Day** (Photo: Ralph Daily, CC BY-SA 2.0)

Casks of bourbon whiskey, for **National Bourbon Day** (Photo: Ken Thomas)

Sarah Vaughan, by William P. Gottlieb — for **AFRICAN-AMERICAN MUSIC APPRECIATION MONTH**

Honorary Months

Presidents, Congresses, and nations around the world issue proclamations recognizing particular months to honor certain causes. These events generally fall in April, though honorary months do come and go.

Holidays established by states and nonprofit organizations are listed if verified. If not otherwise specified, all months are US. There is some variation from year to year; some celebratory months get added and others get dropped. Two places to get up to date information are the current edition of Chase's Calendar of Events *or the website Brownielocks. Here are some honorary designations for June.*

- Adopt-a-Cat Month
- African-American Music Appreciation Month
- Caribbean American Heritage Month
- Children's Awareness Month
- Crop over (Barbados), celebrated until the first Monday in August.
- Dairy Alternative Month
- Fireworks Safety Month
- Gay and Lesbian Pride Month (US)
- Great Outdoors Month (US)
- International Surf Music Month
- Men's Health Education and Awareness Month
- National Accordion Awareness Month
- National Camping Month

- National Rivers Month
- National Safety Month
- National Smile Month (UK)
- National Oceans Month (United States)
- PTSD Awareness Month
- Season of Emancipation (April 14 to August 23) (Barbados)
- Women's Golf Month
- World Naked Bike Ride Month (northern hemisphere)

Just for Fun

Anybody can make up a holiday, and many people do! While none of these are officially recognized and some may come and go, here are a few more holidays for June 14.

- Family History Day
- International Bath Day (celebrates Archimedes' famous bathtub discovery)
- International Surfing Day (third Saturday)
- National Flip Flop Day (third Friday), United States

A 1911 surfer girl, by J. A. Cahill— for **International Surfing Day**

Quote of the Day

"Do you recall that night in June
Upon the Danube River;
We listened to the ländler-tune,
We watched the moonbeams quiver."

— Charles A. Aïdé, "Danube River"

About
the
Month
of
June

June, by Eugène Grasset

June: The Sixth Month

And what is so rare as a day in June?
Then, if ever, come perfect days;
Then Heaven tries earth if it be in tune,
And over it softly her warm ear lays.

— *James Russell Lowell*

In the Julian and Gregorian calendars, June is the sixth month of the year. It's one of the four months that have only 30 days. No months start on the same day of the week as June, an oddity shared only by May. However, June ends on the same day of the week as March in both common and leap years.

In the Northern Hemisphere, June is the month with the longest daylight hours; in the Southern Hemisphere, it's the one with the shortest, equivalent to December. The meteorological summer begins June 21 (the Summer Solstice) in the Northern Hemisphere; the meteorological winter begins on the same day in the Southern Hemisphere (the Winter Solstice).

The English name of June takes its name from the Latin *Iunius*. The poet Ovid gives two theories for the origin of the name. The first is that June is named for the Roman goddess Juno, wife of Jupiter and queen of the gods. The second is that the name comes from the Latin word *iuniores* ("younger ones"), and that the previous month of May comes from *maiores* ("elders")

As the early Roman calendar started its new year in March, June was originally the fourth month of the year. It's uncertain when the Romans switched the new year to January, but it may have been as late as 153 BCE.

June, George Auriol

June in Other Cultures

The month of June has different names in different languages. Some nations use calendars other than the Gregorian, and their months may overlap with June. In lunar-based calendars, such as Islam, months move through the seasons, but they often have a word for June itself.

Albanian: Qershor

Arabic (Egyptian, Sudanese, Moroccan): يونيو (*yūniyū*)

Arabic (Levantine): حزيران (*ḥuzayrān*)

Arabic (Libyan): الصيف (*al-sayf*)

Arabic (Algerian): جوان (*Juwān*)

Azerbaijani: İyun

Basque: Ekain

Bulgarian: юни (*juni*)

Chinese: 六月 (Cantonese: *luhkyuht*; Mandarin: *liùyuè*; Taiwanese: *lak-goeh*)

Corsican: Chjugnu

Czech: červen

Finnish: Kesäkuu

French: Juin

German, Norwegian: Juni

Greek: Ιούνιος (*Ioúnios*)

Hebrew: יוני (*yûnî*)

Hindi: जून (*jūn*)

Hungarian: Június

Irish (Gaelic): Meitheamh mí an Mheithimh

Italian: Giugno

Japanese (traditional calendar): 六月 (*rokugatsu*); 水無月 (*minaduki*)

Korean: 유월 (*yuweol*)

Lithuanian: Birželis

Maori: Pipiri

Old English: Sēremōnaþ

Polish: Czerwiec

Russian: июнь (*ijun'*)

Sesotho: Phupjane

Spanish: Junio

Swedish, Swahili: Juni

Thai: Mithunayon

Vietnamese: 腩𦞌 (tháng sáu)

Welsh: Mehefin

June Brides (and Other Sayings and Superstitions)

June is the most popular month for weddings, followed by August. There are a number of sayings and superstitions about June brides and June weddings.

"A June bride is joyful, jubilant, and jolly well jovial."

"A June bride will be impetuous, and generous."

"Married in the month of roses (June), life will be one long honeymoon."

"Marry when June roses grow, over land and sea you'll go."

"When you marry in June, you'll be a bride all your life." (from the song *June Bride*.)

Which day to get married? That's easy. "Monday for wealth, Tuesday for health, Wednesday the best day of all, Thursday for losses, Friday for crosses, Saturday for no luck at all."

Why such an emphasis on June? Some say it's in honor of Juno, the goddess of marriage. Others suggest it's because back in Medieval days, people would usually have their (yes) annual bath in May, so they'd still be relatively fresh by June. This may also explain the custom of the bridal bouquet.

According to superstition, May is the most unlucky month for marriages, but in ancient Rome the "inauspicious" period ran from May 15 to June 15. The high priestess of Jupiter told the poet Ovid to delay his daughter's wedding until after that date.

There are also some June proverbs for farmers.

"A calm June puts the farmer in tune."

"June damp and warm, does the farmer no harm."

June Symbols

Birthstone Pearl, moonstone, or alexandrite.

Pearl

Moonstone

Alexandrite

Birth Flowers Rose and Honeysuckle

Roses, by Vincent van Gogh

Honeysuckle

                    Michael Dobson

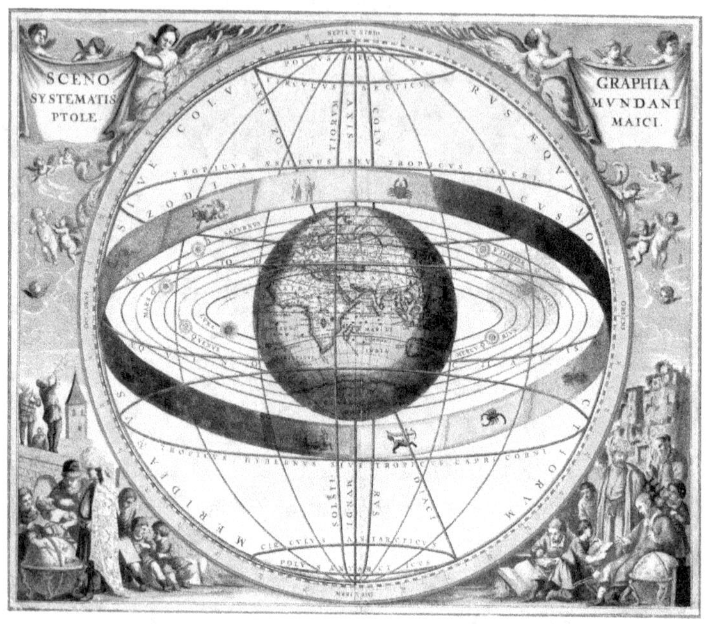

Scenography of the Ptolemaic Cosmography, by Johannes van Loon, based on Andreas Cellarius's *Harmonia Macrocosmica,* 1660

June 14 Zodiac Signs

From the perspective of someone on Earth, the Sun appears to move through the sky throughout the year, along a path astronomers call the *ecliptic plane*. The ecliptic plane is divided into twelve constellations, known as the zodiac, based on traditionally observed patterns of stars. On your birthday, you can't see your constellation, because it's in the daytime sky.

The zodiac was first developed by Babylonian astronomers about 2,500 years ago. Because they were unaware that the Earth wobbles like a spinning top (known as *precession*), they didn't make allowance for the fact that the Sun's path through the zodiac changes over time.

That means there are now two sets of dates for your birth sign. The *tropical dates* are the original Babylonian dates; the *sidereal dates* tell you where the Sun actually appears as it moves along its annual path.

For June 14, the tropical sign is **Gemini** and the sidereal sign is **Taurus.**

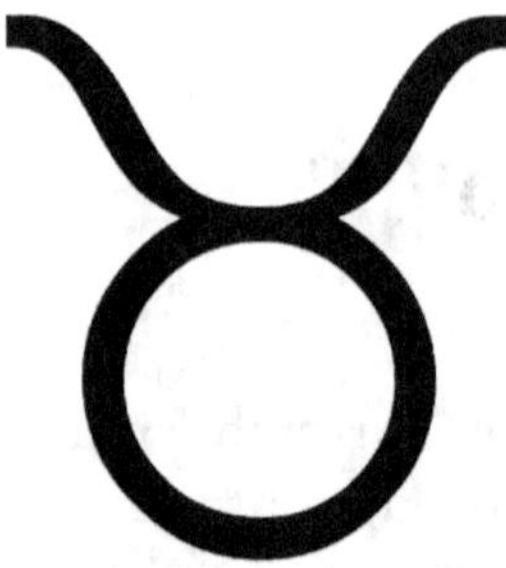

Taurus

Tropical April 21 to May 22
Siderial May 16 to June 15

In Greek mythology, Taurus was a disguise adopted by Zeus, who appeared to the maiden Europa in the form of a gentle white bull. Europa unwisely got too close, and Zeus kidnapped her to the island of Crete, where she bore him three sons, including Minos, builder of the labyrinth that housed the minotaur.

In astrology, Taurus is an earth sign, and Taureans are supposed to be quiet, gentle, compassionate, and stubborn. Taureans can appreciate the finer things in life and are cautious with money.

Gemini

Tropical May 22 to June 21
Sidereal June 16 to July 15

According to Greek mythology, Leda, wife of the King of Sparta, gave birth to Helen of Troy and Clytemnestra. The god Zeus, disguised as a swan, seduced her after she had already lain with her husband on the same night. This resulted in two eggs, which hatched to become the twins Castor and Pollux. Castor's father was the King of Sparta, but Pollux was the son of Zeus and therefore immortal. When Castor died, Pollux shared his immortality, so that they could divide their time between Hades and Olympus. They were enshrined in the Zodiac as the constellation Gemini, the Twins.

In astrology, Gemini is an air sign, ruled by Mercury, compatible with Libra, Aquarius, and Aries. Geminis are supposed to be communicative, flexible, intellectual, and curious, but prone to fickleness and easily distracted.

Illustration by Edward Penfield

What Day of the Week is June 14?

On what day of the week does June 14 fall?

Surprisingly, this isn't an easy question. Because the calendar year is 365 days long (366 in leap years), it doesn't divide evenly by the seven days of the week.

Also, the Earth goes around the Sun in about 365-1/4 days, so a calendar tends to drift over time. That's why the same date falls on different weekdays in different years.

This is made even more complicated by a change in calendars that took place in 1582. Our modern calendar has its roots in ancient Rome, in a calendar reform conducted by Julius Caesar. Caesar commissioned mathematicians to attack the problem, and they came up with the idea of leap years, and thus standardized the calendar for centuries to come. This was called the Julian calendar.

Over time, however, the small errors in Caesar's calculation compounded. That's why Pope Gregory XIII commissioned the Gregorian calendar, used in most of the world today. Some countries converted in 1582, when the calendar was first developed; some converted later; other still haven't changed.

Gregorian and Julian aren't the only types of calendars. The Hebrew year, the Islamic year, and many other calendars are used in different parts of the world and among different people.

You can convert Gregorian dates to other calendars, including the Hebrew calendar, the Islamic calendar, and even the Mayan calendar by visiting the Fourmilab Calendar Converter at http://www.fourmilab.ch/documents/calendar/.

Chinese calendar systems are quite complex and have changed several times; a full discussion is far beyond the scope of this book. If you're interested, you can find information here: http://www.hermetic.ch/cal_stud/chinese_cal.htm.

On Names and Dates

Historians use "CE" (Common Era) and "BCE" (Before the Common Era) instead of the more common "AD" (Anno Domini, or Year of Our Lord) and "BC" (Before Christ), reflecting the fact that the year-numbering system established by the Gregorian calendar is used throughout the world in many countries not culturally Christian.

The CE/BCE designation dates back to at least 1708, and has been adopted as a standard by the United Nations and the Universal Postal Union. Because this series of books covers events and people of all nations and cultures, we use the CE/BCE terms.

The abbreviation "O.S." ("Old Style") and "N.S." ("New Style") on some dates refers to the fact that the Russian Empire (in particular) did not switch from the Julian to the Gregorian calendar at the same time as the rest of Europe, and therefore some figures and events have two dates.

Also, in the Julian calendar in England in the 16th century, the year began on March 25 rather than January 1. To avoid confusion with Gregorian dates, dates between January and March were often written using both years.

People and events whose original names are not in the Western alphabet have their native names (where possible) in the appropriate script shown in parenthesis. If you are using an e-reader to access an electronic version of this book, all characters don't always display on all devices.

A 50-year brass perpetual calendar.

Quote of the Day

"Time is an illusion, lunchtime doubly so."

Douglas Adams,
from *The Hitchhiker's Guide to the Galaxy*

Notes
and
Credits
THEIR
ACC
MAGNA
Timespinner
Press

Cartoon by John T. McCutcheon

Copyright, Credit, and Contact

Follow Us

Our blog "This Day in History" (http://
timespinnerpress.com/this-day-in-history/) features short
articles on events and people associated with each day, and
updates several times each week. Also subscribe to the
"Quote of the Day" at http://timespinnerpress.com/quote-
of-the-day/. You can get daily links by following us on
Facebook at TimespinnerPress, or on Twitter as
@sidewisethinker.

Contact Us

Find an error or a format problem? Want information about
the series, about us, or about when the volume for your
special day might be available? Please email us at
editor@timespinnerpress.com. (We also take requests if your
special day isn't yet complete. Please give us at least six
weeks' notice if possible.)

Sources

We owe a great debt to Wikipedia, which is our first stop for
research. We attempt to make independent confirmation of
all important dates and facts through a variety of other
sources.

Other sources we frequently use include the Library of
Congress; "on this day" listings from *Encyclopedia Britannica,*
the *New York Times,* and the BBC; Omniglot for the names of
months in other languages; *Chase's Calendar of Events;* and, of
course, the always essential Google.

All art and photographs are either in the public domain, used under a Creative Commons license, or with a "fair use" justification, and most frequently come from Wikimedia Commons and the Library of Congress Prints and Photographs Division.

Attribution is provided where possible, or as requested by the copyright owner, or when there is particular historical significance, listed below. For information about any particular illustration or photograph, please contact us.

Credits

1. The painting of Betsy Ross by Jean Leon Gerome Ferris is from the collection of the Library of Congress, digital ID cph. 3g09905. Because the painter died in 1930, the work is in the public domain in the United States, its country of origin, and other countries and areas where the copyright term is the author's life plus eighty years or less. It has been cropped to fit the dimensions of the cover.

2. The illustration of the month of June used on the back cover is from the French Gothic illuminated manuscript *Les Très Riches Heures du duc de Berry* by the Limbourg Brothers, Jean Colombe, and an intermediate painter whose name is lost to history. It is in the public domain because its copyright has expired.

3. The box graphic used on the first page is from a 1916 pamphlet entitled "Divorce versus Democracy" authored by G. K. Chesterton, originally published in London by the Society of St. Peter and St. Paul. It is in the public domain in the US because it was published prior to 1923, and is in the public domain in all countries (including the country of origin) in which the copyright time is the author's life plus 70 years or less.

4. The graphic design for the section pages in this book is from a design originally created for a pharmacy label. It is courtesy of Wellcome Images (ICV No 11073, photo V0010813), and is used here under CC BY-SA 4.0.

5. The illustration "The Mutineers turning Lt. Bligh and part of the Officers and Crew adrift from His Majesty's Ship the Bounty" was first published in 1790 and is in the public domain because its copyright has expired. It is in the National Maritime Museum, Greenwich, London (accession number PAH9205).

6. The June 14, 1919, photograph of Alcock and Brown prior to takeoff is from the collection of Library and Archives Canada (PA-121930). It is in the public domain in Canada because it was published more than 50 years ago, and in the US because it was first published prior to January 1, 1923.

7. The 1991 photograph of a monorail at Disneyland was taken by David Jones, and is used here under CC BY-SA 2.0.

8. The photograph of Harriet Beecher Stowe was taken sometime between 1870 and 1890, and is in the public domain because its copyright has expired. It is in the collection of the US National Archives and Records Administration, NAID 535784. The photographer is unknown.

9. The 2017 photograph of President Donald Trump at the Pentagon was taken by USAF SSGT Jette Carr. It is in the public domain as a work created by an employee of the US government as part of that person's official duties.

10. The 1937 photograph "Kentucky Flood" is, to the best of our knowledge, still under copyright. It is used here under "fair use" provisions of the copyright law. It is an important image to illustrate the career of the photographer, no equivalent free image exists, and the size and quality of the reproduction is too low to allow the creation of counterfeit goods. No challenge to the copyright holder is intended.

11. The 1959 photograph of Che Guevara is in the public domain in Cuba, its country of origin because it is more than 25 years old. It is in the public domain in the US because it was first published in Cuba before February 20, 1972, without compliance with US copyright laws.

12. The 1958 publicity photograph of Gene Barry from the television series *Bat Masterson* is in the public domain because it was published in the United States between 1923 and 1977 without a copyright notice. Traditionally, publicity

photographs are not copyrighted because of the way in which they are intended to be used.

13. The 1955 photograph of Burl Ives by Carl Van Vechten is in the public domain because it was published in the United States between 1923 and 1977 without a copyright notice. It is from the collection of the Library of Congress, digital ID van.5a52165.

14. The 1916 photograph from the film *Big Tremaine* is in the public domain because its copyright has expired.

15. The 1907 photograph of Jacob Ellehammer's triplane is in the collection of the Metropolitan Museum of Art, New York, and has been made available by the museum under the CC0 1.0 Universal Public Domain Dedication, releasing it entirely into the public domain.

16. The 2012 photograph of Steffi Graf by Chris Eason is used here under CC BY-SA 2.0.

17. The 1878 self-portrait of Mary Cassatt is in the public domain because its copyright has expired. It is in the collection of the Metropolitan Museum of Art, accession number 1975.319.1.

18. The 1880s photograph of the Home Insurance Building, Chicago, is in the collections of the Library of Congress, digital ID mhsalad.250058. It is in the public domain because its copyright has expired.

19. The drawing "Plan of the City of Washington" by Pierre L'Enfant was revised by Andrew Ellicott in 1792. It is in the public domain because its copyright has expired.

20. The 1914 photograph "Mrs Emmeline Pankhurst, Leader of the Women's Suffragette movement, is arrested outside Buckingham Palace while trying to present a petition to King George V in May 1914" is in the public domain because its copyright has expired. It is in the public domain as a work created by the United Kingdom Government taken prior to June 1, 1957, and in the public domain in the United States because it was created prior to January 1, 1923. It is from the collections of the Imperial War Museum, photograph Q 81486.

21. The 1879 engraving of Benedict Arnold by Henry Bryan Hall (after John Trumbull) is in the public domain because its copyright has expired.

22. The photograph of The Ventures originally appeared in a trade ad in *Billboard* magazine, page 11, April 29, 1967. is in the public domain because it was published in the United States between 1923 and 1977 without a copyright notice.

23. The photograph of John Logie Baird was taken in 1925 by Orrin Dunlap, Jr., and published in *Popular Radio* magazine in 1926. It is in the public domain because it was published in the United States between 1923 and 1963 and although there may or may not have been a copyright notice, the copyright was not renewed.

24. The poster for the 1917 Flag Day celebration is from the collection of the Library of Congress, digital ID cph.3g06262. It is in the public domain because its copyright has expired.

25. The 1919 photograph of the first Flag Day celebration at the US Capitol is in the public domain as a work created by an employee of the US government (Office of the Architect of the Capitol) as part of that person's official duties.

26. The 2007 photograph of a father wearing a necktie cookie is by Dean Michaud, and is used here under CC BY-SA 2.0.

27. The 2014 photograph of a strawberry-Grand Marnier shortcake at Chez Fonfon in Birmingham, Alabama, was taken by Ralph Daily, and is used here under CC BY-SA 2.0.

28. The 2013 photograph of barrels of bourbon at the Woodford Reserve, Versailles, Kentucky, was taken by Ken Thomas, who released the work into the public domain.

29. The 1946 photograph of Sarah Vaughan was taken by William P. Gottlieb, and is part of the William P. Gottlieb Collection of jazz photographs at the Library of Congress. In accordance with the wishes of Gottlieb, the photographs in the collection entered into the public domain in 2010.

30. The July 1911 cover of *Sunset* magazine, painted by J. A. Cahill, is in the public domain because it was first published prior to January 1, 1923, and its copyright has expired.

31. The 1896 drawing "June" by Eugène Grasset is in the public domain because its copyright has expired.

32. The 1912 graphic of June by George Auriol is in the public domain because its copyright has expired.

33. The 1815 woodcut of a proposal is in the public domain because its copyright has expired.

34. The photo of a pearl necklace is by "Anna reg," taken from Wikimedia Commons and used here under CC BY-SA 3.0.

35. The photograph of a Brazilian moonstone is by Didier Descouens, taken from Wikimedia Commons and used here under CC BY-SA 4.0.

36. The photograph of alexandrite under ultraviolet light is by Parent Géry, taken from Wikimedia Commons and used here because the creator has dedicated the rights to the public domain under CC0 1.0.

37. The painting *Roses* by Vincent Van Gogh can be found in the collection of the National Gallery of Art, Washington, DC. The image is in the public domain because its copyright has expired.

38. The illustration of honeysuckle originally appeared in the book *American Homes and Gardens*, published by Munn & Co., New York, in 1905. It is in the public domain because its copyright has expired. The image was taken from Flickr's The Commons.

39. The celestial sphere is from *Scenography of the Ptolemaic Cosmography*, by Johannes van Loon, based on Andreas Cellarius's *Harmonia Macrocosmica*, 1660. It is in the public domain because its copyright has expired.

40. The 1906 automobile calendar is by Edward Penfield, and is in the collection of the Library of Congress Prints and Photographs Division. It is in the public domain because its copyright has expired.

41. The 50-year perpetual calendar photograph is in the public domain.

42. The cartoon by John T. McCutcheon is from his 1905 collection *The Mysterious Stranger and Other Cartoons by John T. McCutcheon*. It is in the public domain because its copyright has expired.

43. The painting "June" by Simon Bening is from the *Brevarium Grimani*, circa 1510, and is in the public domain because its copyright has expired.

44. The painting "June" by Hans Thoma is from his book *Festkalender*. It is in the public domain because it was published prior to 1923 and its copyright has expired.

License Description and Terms

Aside from material purely in the public domain, photographs and other material in this book are used under specific licenses permitting free use, usually with an attribution requirement. For full text and terms of these licenses, click or enter the appropriate links below. If you believe there is an error in the copyright status or attribution of any of these images, please email us.

- Creative Commons Attribution 2.0 Generic (CC-BY 2.0): http://creativecommons.org/licenses/by/2.0/deed.en
- Creative Commons Attribution-Share Alike 3.0 Generic (CC-BY-SA 3.0): http://creativecommons.org/licenses/by-sa/3.0/
- Creative Commons Attribution-Share Alike 2.5 Generic (CC-BY-SA 2.5): http://creativecommons.org/licenses/by-sa/2.5/deed.en
- Creative Commons Attribution-Share Alike 2.0 Generic (CC-BY-SA 2.0): http://creativecommons.org/licenses/by/2.0/deed.en
- Creative Commons Attribution-Share Alike 1.0 Generic (CC-BY-SA 1.0): http://creativecommons.org/licenses/by-sa/1.0/deed.en
- CC0 1.0 Universal (CC0 1.0) Public Domain Dedication (CC0 1.0) http://creativecommons.org/publicdomain/zero/1.0/deed.en
- GNU Free Documentation License (GFDL): http://en.wikipedia.org/wiki/Wikipedia:Text_of_the_GNU_Free_Documentation_License
- License Art Libre (Free Art License): http://artlibre.org

Timespinner
Press

"June," from the *Brevarium Grimani* by Simon Bening (c.1510)

Other Books from Timespinner Press

The Story of a Special Day
Michael Dobson

A series of (eventually) 366 volumes covering everything that happened on your special day! Events, births, deaths, quotes, holidays, and much more. It's like a birthday card they'll never throw away!

US$7.95 print / US$2.99 ebook.

From Plassey to Pakistan
Humayun Mirza

The history of British Colonial India and the formation of Pakistan from the unique perspective of the son of Pakistan's first president and last of the royal line of Bengal, Bihar, and Orissa! This unique historical document tells the inside story of this distinguished family, including the detailed story of the coup that toppled his father from power!

US$27.95 print

A Whole New Navy: America's War in the Pacific

Miles Durr

The most comprehensive and detailed description of America's naval war in the Pacific ever—every battle, every ship, every task force and every task group from Pearl Harbor through the Japanese surrender! A must-have for the collection of every World War II buff!

US$29.95 print

Improbable History: The Weird, the Obscure, and the Strangely Important

edited by Michael Dobson

From the birth of Western civilization to the rescue of Apollo 13, from the Leaning Tower of Pisa to Florence's Duomo, history has often turned on small, improbable details. Whatever happened to the ancient Samaritan people? Why did a fortuitous rainstorm allow the British to conquer India? How did an air raid in Italy lead to the development of chemotherapy? What happened when Albert Einstein met Adolf Hitler on the streets of Berlin? How did the Japanese manage to attack the US mainland using balloons? A cast of award-winning writers tackle some of the strangest tales in history!

US$19.95 print

The Letters of William Philip Schwartz 1842-1855

edited by John F. Schwartz

The 19th century soldier and adventurer William Philip Schwartz wrote a series of vivid and detailed letters chronicling his adventures in the Indian Wars, the Mexican-American War, the Gold Rush, and his term as Marine sergeant aboard the USS Constellation. A pioneer in photography, he took *the first known war photographs*. An unforgettable first-hand look into life in the 19th century!

US$17.95 print

Timespinner
Press

www.timespinnerpress.com

June, by Hans Thoma